cinderly

PRODUCED BY Cinderly, Inc.

CREATIVE DIRECTOR Luke Stoffel
EDITOR Mayumi Shimose Poe
ASSISTANT EDITOR Laura von Holt
BAKING ASSISTANT Cynthia Wang
ASSISTANT FOOD STYLIST Alys Arden

SPECIAL THANKS TO

Jess Ochoa, Joyce Stoffel, Heidi Kroner, John Allen Pierce, Andrew Douglas, Taylor Harris, Eric Kim, Nansi Schneider, Steve Young, Darcy Lawton, Kim Hale, Amanda Jaskiewicz McLellan, Cyndi Gryte, Erin Clark, Jerry Wong, Jenny Thrinh, Carrie Ferguson Pazdol, Daniel Beaver-Seitz, and Michelle Ulness.

IN LOVING MEMORY OF

Ethan Adi Guidjaja, Aggie Stoffel, and Helen Sahm.

cinderly's

easy to bake
Unicorn
Cookbook

www.unicorncookbook.com

Don't Quit Your Daydream

I grew up baking in my mom's cherry-colored kitchen, my little sister and I carefully following the instructions on a set of worn paper cards from my grandmother's recipe box. My family raised us on the banks of the Mississippi River, and the tradition of sweets ran about as deep in us as that river is long. So when I dreamed of my sure-to-be colorful future, it was frequently filled with the vision of running my own Rainbow Cake Café. For me the most important part of living my life to its fullest potential was finding a way to share my glitter-covered, creative impulses with the world.

While visiting my cousin down in New Orleans, I learned that she'd spent the last few years as a sous chef at a delightfully inspired pastry shop in the French Quarter called Sucre. She said one of her greatest sources of joy was still baking, and it was then that I realized the true depth of our grandmother's influence on all of our lives. When I returned to New York, I began bringing to life some of my favorite childhood recipes of hers, with my own sense of color, style, and fervor influencing them.

I hope my grandma is looking on from above, thinking that all of her grandchildren have made her proud.

Chief Executive Belieber

Luke Stoffel - Cinderly, Inc.

Egg-cellent Pro Tips

We hope these stories and recipes inspire a lifelong love of baking in the kitchen with your family. May the memories you make there be passed down for generations, just as I pass them from my grandmother to you.

Here are a few egg-cellent tips before you start! The eggs are always large, the butter is always unsalted. If it says "softened" then wait until it's at room temperature otherwise everything will be lumpy. Butter will always taste better, but we sometimes use Crisco because it makes the food coloring more vibrant. Try to use self-rising flour (cake flour) when noted, otherwise all-purpose flour is fine. General rule of thumb, stick a toothpick in the center of a cake to test its readiness; if it comes out clean, it's done! Everything will taste great as long as you had fun, and if you feel woefully worried, never underestimate the power of frosting to fix!

Tag your creations **#UnicornCookbook** on Instagram and let the rainbow baking battles begin!

EASY BAKE OPTIONS:

For a guide to buy all of our favorite cookie cutters, sprinkles, shortcuts, and Easy Bake options, please visit: **UnicornCookbook.com**

Slumber Party Popcorn Balls

When visions of sugar plums don't dance in your head... it's probably because you didn't feed that head enough sugar before bed!

For me and my little sister, Friday nights were for slumber parties, movies in the basement, and creating our own makeshift roller rink on the neighbors' cement slab in their backyard. There was always a table nearby covered in pizza and treats, and the memory of those Friday nights will forever be scented with the smells of popcorn and cherry gelatin!

EASY BAKE OPTION:

Ask your mom to do it for you and go find a movie to watch. LOL.
There is no easy-bake option for this recipe, it's pretty easy as is.

Slumber Party Popcorn Balls

WHAT YOU WILL NEED:

1 CUP White corn syrup
1 CUP Sugar
1 PACKAGE (3 oz.) flavored gelatin or Jell-o
9 CUPS Popped popcorn

THE STEP BY STEP:

STEP 1   Set aside popped popcorn in a large bowl.

STEP 2   Grab a large pot and add 1 cup white corn syrup, 1 cup sugar, and 1 package flavored gelatin. We love cherry.

STEP 3   Mix all ingredients except popcorn on medium/high heat.

STEP 4   Bring mixture to a boil, and cook until gelatin and sugar are totally dissolved.

STEP 5   Pour mixture over popcorn and stir well with large rubber spatula.

STEP 6   Coat your hands in Butter (or Crisco), and quickly grab the covered popcorn and form it into balls, any size.

STEP 7   Place the finished balls on wax paper and once cooled wrap them in plastic wrap or serve as is.

DECORATING TIP:

For an ombre effect, separate the popcorn into 3 batches.

Follow the instructions as noted, but add the gelatin in 3 parts to the clear mixture so that each bowl of popcorn becomes darker as you add more gelatin.

Add 1 part gelatin to the clear mixture, and pour 1/3 of the mixture on your first batch of popcorn. It should appear light pink. Add 2nd part of gelatin to remaining clear mixture so the second batch of popcorn becomes a darker pink. Finally add your last part of gelatin to the remaining mixture and coat your third batch of popcorn so it is a bright red color.

For the ultimate in unicorn decorating, add candy hearts or star sprinkles to the balls before they cool.

Slumber Party Popcorn Balls

Birthday Buttercream

Let's be honest, there ain't nothing better or more useful in the kitchen than a bowl full of buttercream frosting. It seems like we always need it for something. It's a staple in any baker's kitchen, but we dressed it up to be the star it is!

WHAT YOU WILL NEED:

4 CUPS Powdered sugar
½ CUP Crisco (or softened butter)
1 TEASPOON Vanilla
6 TABLESPOONS Milk as needed

THE STEP BY STEP:

Gather 4 cups powdered sugar in a large mixing bowl. Then add ½ cup Crisco (or softened butter) to the bowl and 1 teaspoon of vanilla and run mixer on low until ingredients start to blend.

Keep mixer running and add milk slowly, 1 tablespoon at a time until the mixture is soft. If your frosting is too thick, beat the concoction on high and continue to add more milk. It should start to become smooth and form stiff peaks when you lift up the mixer.

EASY BAKE OPTION:

Just grab a tub of white frosting from the store. We love to use Wilton® White Ready To Use Decorator Icing (readily available on Amazon)!

Bunny Batter Cake

Springtime in Iowa marked my oldest sister's birthday. Jelly Bellies®
flowed throughout all our bedrooms. One of my most vivid memories
is of sitting with her and my mom in the kitchen making her a very
special birthday cake. My mother would call out into the living room
to the herd of children huddled around the TV that she was cooking
up some Bunny Batter and if anyone wanted to pitch in, they'd
better hurry up!

I loved this time of year because a sugarfest exploded in our house
like we had opened a local chocolatier. For my sister, the birthday
girl, there was always one giant chocolate egg waiting for her in
a pristine box from the candy store downtown, right next to her
coconut-flavored bunny cake.

EASY BAKE OPTION:

For a simpler way to make this recipe, grab of box of white cake mix at the store
and follow the instructions on the box! Then pick up with the instructions in the
Decorating Tips section on the next page.

Bunny Batter Cake

WHAT YOU WILL NEED:

2 LARGE Egg whites

1 CUP Sugar

2 TEASPOON Vanilla extract

1 CUP Self-rising flour

2 TABLESPOONS Powdered Chai tea (optional)

2 TEASPOON Baking powder

½ TEASPOON Salt

¼ CUP Vegetable or Canola Oil

½ CUP Milk

½ CUP Hot water (boiling)

1 BAG Coconut flakes

3 PIECES Jellybeans (2 black, 1 pink)

THE STEP BY STEP:

STEP 1   Preheat the oven to 350°F; meanwhile in a large mixing bowl, beat 2 egg whites with a hand mixer. Then slowly add 1 cup sugar, and 1 teaspoon vanilla extract and continue to beat for 3 minutes.

STEP 2   Gradually fold into the wet mixture 1 cup flour, 2 tablespoons powdered chai tea powdered milk (if desired), 2 teaspoon baking powder, and ½ teaspoon salt.

STEP 3   Add ¼ cup oil, and ½ cup milk, stir, and mix in ½ cup hot water. You can place the water in the microwave for 2 minutes, or until it boils. Don't worry, the batter will be thin. This is correct.

STEP 4   Grease and pour batter into one 9-inch cake pan. Bake for 30 minutes. If you have extra batter pour into a cupcakes tin and bake for 20 minutes.

DECORATING TIPS:

Make a batch of buttercream frosting (recipe can be found on page 13). An easy alternative is to use a store-bought white frosting.

Cool and cut the 9-inch round cake in half, so that you have two half-circles. Add frosting to the flat side of one of the cakes. Then combine the two halves together, so your cake looks like a half circle sandwich. Place the cut bottoms flat on the table, so the half circle sandwich sits straight up to form the body of the bunny.

Coat and frost the entire standing cake with leftover buttercream— there is no need to be perfect. To form the bunny's legs, cut one cupcake in quarters and glue one quarter to the rear of each side and cover with frosting.

Coat the entire cake with coconut flakes, then add two black jelly beans for eyes and one pink one for the nose. (Alternately, we used a pink M&M for a round-shaped nose.)

Using pink or white construction paper, cut out two long ear shapes and gently curl together and place in the top of the cake.

No-Bake Mermaid Cheesecake

Summers in Iowa are hot and the only way to cool off is to go down by the river. Whether you were fishing for catfish, running from dragon flies, or sitting out back of the Dairy Queen eating soft serve, the easy breeze of river life is a staple on the Mississippi.

One summer my niece and I were running from the blistering heat of the July sun, when we grabbed my little sister and headed straight on over to the beauty supply shop. You see the only way grandma would let us stay inside was if we had something to do, so we hastily decided to set this summer off in style and started dyeing my niece's hair in miraculous mermaid fashion. The whole afternoon was a glorious mess of stained blue and purple fingers. But even before we did a final rinse to reveal her instagram-worthy hair, Grandma was already screeching as she tried to scrub toxic goo off the base of her ruined white tub.

I'd never say our calling in life was to be hairstylists, but for a few days anyway my niece's hair did look as lovely as this No-Bake Mermaid Cheesecake, which we promptly set to work on after the whole hair-dye fiasco was put to bed.

EASY BAKE OPTION:

Grab a pre-made graham cracker crust and a no-bake cheesecake mix from the store. Follow the instructions and then start at step 3 on the next page.

No-Bake Mermaid Cheesecake

WHAT YOU WILL NEED:

2 BLOCKS 8 oz. cream cheese, softened
1 CUP Sugar
2 CUPS Heavy cream
4 BOTTLES AmeriColor food dye, in sky blue, teal, purple & pink
1 CRUST Graham cracker

THE STEP BY STEP:

STEP 1 Take your cream cheese out of the fridge and keep at room temperature. Use your hand mixer to beat 2 blocks of cream cheese alone first, then slowly add sugar until smooth. Cream cheese will become lumpy if it hasn't been warmed.

STEP 2 Mix in 2 cups of heavy cream and beat until the mixture is stiff and forms peaks. I'd say at least 3 minutes.

STEP 3 Divide batter into 4 small bowls, and add several drops of a single food color to each bowl—sky blue, teal, purple, and pink. Mix well!

STEP 4 Take your crust and spoon in large portions of the colored mixtures, alternating colors until you've used all the mixture. We did a layer of blue and teal, and a layer of pink and purple.

STEP 5 Cover with sprinkles and place in the refrigerator for 6 to 8 hours, till cheesecake becomes firm.

DECORATING TIPS:

Before you take your cheesecake out of the fridge, prepare your whip cream. Using one small container of Cool Whip® from the store, stir in sky blue food coloring. Stir until whip cream becomes entirely sky blue and scoop it into a piping bag or frosting tool of your choice.

Remove cheesecake from the fridge, add additional sprinkles, and top with light blue dollops of cool whip.

For extra fun, we also like to add giant white chocolate pearls to give this decadent treat an extra-special glow.

No-Bake Mermaid Cheesecake

Lil' Monster Brownies

In Iowa you don't trick-or-treat with a orange bucket that looks like a pumpkin. You go up to your bedroom, tear the pillow cases off your bed, and then you ransack the town! My brothers established a very well-worn trick-or-treat route that always looted us the best and fullest lot of candy! We would hurry home after filling our pillowsacks so much that we could hardly lug them down the block and unload them on to the living room floor. We then ran upstairs, ripped the largest drawer from our dresser, flinging undergarments to all corner of the room, and used the emptied space to sort our candy into rainbow-ordered rows. After all in the face of so much glorious, color-coated indulgence, socks were pretty useless.

Because we had such an overflow of candy in the house, my mother always would find a creative way to use it. Embedding it into brownies was of course the BEST way to do that!

EASY BAKE OPTION:

Buy a box of brownie mix and some chocolate frosting. Follow the instructions on the box, then follow our decorating tips on the next page!

Lil' Monster Brownies

WHAT YOU WILL NEED:

2 LARGE Eggs

1 TEASPOON Vanilla extract

1 CUP Sugar

½ **CUP** Unsalted butter (softened)

¼ **TEASPOON** Baking powder

½ **CUP** Cocoa

½ **CUP** All-purpose flour

¼ **TEASPOON** Salt

¼ **CUP** Hershey's® syrup

THE STEP BY STEP:

STEP 1 Preheat the oven to 350°F. Then grab 2 large eggs, 1 teaspoon vanilla extract, 1 cup sugar, and ½ cup butter then beat with a hand mixer for 3 minutes until creamy.

STEP 2 Add ¼ teaspoon baking powder, ½ cup cocoa, ½ cup flour, ¼ teaspoon salt, ¼ cup Hershey's® syrup, and continue to mix until combined.

STEP 3 Using butter (or Crisco), grease a 9 x 9 inch square pan, then add a handful of flour and coat all sides.

STEP 4 Place into the oven for 20 minutes. To check if the brownies are done, you can stick a toothpick in them. They're done when the toothpick comes out clean.

STEP 5 Cool completely before cutting.

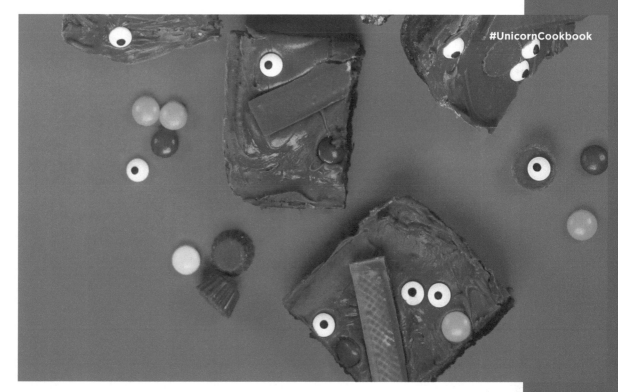

DECORATING TIPS:

After the brownies cool, top with Poo Party Chocolate Frosting (recipe can be found on page 51) or use store-bought chocolate frosting and fully coat the top of the brownies while still in the pan.

Directly after frosting, place pieces of Kit Kat® bar, Reese's Pieces®, and peanut butter cups on top of the frosting. Press down on the candy so it is firmly nudged into the frosting.

Grab a set of Wilton® candied eyeballs (available at your local Target store or on Amazon) and place in key spots to make your brownies extra creepy!

Lil' Monster Brownies

Valentine Blondies

I don't know how it is for you, but Valentine's Day was always a big deal when I was a kid. Everyone in the classroom would decorate large paper bags with cut-out hearts and colorful markers. Our teachers would tape them to the back of our chairs, and they would fill up throughout the day. It was always a treat to get home from school with a bag full of My Little Pony® love notes and candy hearts.

These days, my mailbox still flows full on Valentine's Day with beautiful handmade cards from my mom and my sister. In fact, the paper heart in the picture was the valentine my sister and her kids sent me last year. And though I still love the outpouring of support from others, I also like to do something for myself each year. On one such year, on an overly grey February day in New York, with the snowy sludge piled high on the streets, this recipe was reborn. And then it was cut into hearts and adorned with all the pink and red I could find in my kitchen!

Remember: On Valentine's Day, love others, but also love your selfie.

EASY BAKE OPTION:

Buy a tub of frozen chocolate chip cookie dough. Flatten and place in a 9 x 9 inch pan, press candies and butterscotch chips into the top. Then bake 18–20 minutes and cut into shapes.

Valentine Blondies

¾ **CUP** White sugar

¾ **CUP** Packed brown sugar

½ **CUP** Softened butter (or Crisco)

2 LARGE Eggs

1 TEASPOON Vanilla extract

1 ½ CUPS All-purpose flour

½ **TEASPOON** Baking powder

½ **TEASPOON** Salt

½ **CUP** Semisweet chocolate chips

½ **CUP** Butterscotch chips

½ **CUP** M&M's®

THE STEP BY STEP:

STEP 1   Preheat the over to 350°. Then in a large bowl, combine ¾ cup white sugar, ¾ cup brown sugar, ½ cup butter, 2 eggs, and 1 teaspoon vanilla extract. With a hand mixer on medium high, mix until blended and creamy.

STEP 2   Combine the 1 ½ cups of flour, ½ teaspoon baking powder, and ½ teaspoon salt; add to the cream mixture. Next fold in ½ cup chocolate chips, ½ cup butterscotch chips, and ½ cup M&M's®. (Save a few M&M's® for decorating the top.)

STEP 3   Spread batter into a greased 9x9-inch baking pan and press a handful of additional M&M's® into the top of the batter. Bake for 18–20 minutes.

STEP 4   Cool for 30 minutes before cutting into bars or shapes.

DECORATING TIPS:

We love decorating with pink and red M&M's® and cutting into hearts, but this amazing treat can be served many different ways.

Feel free to bake the blondie batter in a 9-inch round greased cake pan and decorate with chocolate frosting, sprinkles, and rainbow M&M's® for a giant birthday cookie! Then cut and serve in triangles like pizza!

Valentine Blondies

Sea Salt Pretzel Sticks

In my house, *The Little Mermaid* was the most important movie of our childhood. I think me and my little sis watched the VHS tape so many times that it finally wore out. ("VHS" is what we watched movies on before streaming.) Seeing as how every time we sat down to watch the movie, we would recite every single word of the Disney classic, you know we needed the appropriate refreshments. These pretzel sticks, bathed in white chocolate and adorned with sprinkles and goldfish crackers, hit all the right notes of salty and sweet. Plus, "I love little fishes, don't you?"

WHAT YOU WILL NEED:

1 BOX Pretzel sticks
1 BAG White chocolate chips or candy melts (any color)
1 BAG Goldfish crackers
1 BOTTLE Sprinkles

THE STEP BY STEP:

Melt white chocolate or candy melts in the microwave or stove top, stirring every 30 seconds for no more than 2 minutes. Once completely melted, add additional food coloring (if desired) and mix until color is consistent.

Dip pretzel into the chocolate mixture, then spoon chocolate over the pretzel stick until half covered. Then add sprinkles of your choice on top, and afix 2 goldfish at the top and the bottom. Place on wax paper to cool.

Continue to cover pretzels until all of the chocolate mixture is finished.

Peeps® Pizza

This new classic is an homage to my mother. All the grandkids know that Grandma Joyce loves Peeps® marshmallow bunnies! Every year she gets more Peeps® memorabilia, Peeps® pajamas, collector's boxes, and more! One year I even went to the Peeps® headquarters in Bethlehem, Pennsylvania, to bring her home some special football-sized marshmallow peep treats! So needless to say when thinking about our ultimate unicorn treats, I had to spend a little extra love on this one.

We hereby humbly bestow upon your household the best pizza recipe this side of Delaware River! We love this one so much we even keep a stash of Peeps® in our pantry for special occasions!

EASY BAKE OPTION:

In a microwave-safe bowl, heat ½ stick of butter and 15 large marshmallows on high for 2 minutes. Stir. If ingredients are not mixing well, heat for another minute until smooth. While stirring, add 3 cups of Rice Krispies® and press into a round cake pan.

Peeps® Pizza

WHAT YOU WILL NEED:

¼ **CUP** Butter

2 CUPS Marshmallows large or small

3 CUPS Rice Krispies® cereal

1 PACKAGE Marshmallow Peeps®

1 BOTTLE Food coloring (optional)

THE STEP BY STEP:

STEP 1 In large pot or saucepan, melt ¼ cup of butter over low heat. Add in 2 cups of marshmallows, and stir until everything is completely melted. Then remove from heat.

STEP 2 Using a rubber spatula (you can smear it with butter to prevent sticking) to stir, add 2 drops of food coloring (if desired) and 3 cups of Rice Krispies® cereal. Stir until well coated.

STEP 3 Press the treats into a greased 9-inch round cake pan and top with sprinkles. Let cool.

TIP At my house, one of these delectable pizzas was never enough. I definitely recommend doubling the pizza for twice the fun!

DECORATING TIPS:

Grab a tub of store-bought white frosting and add green food color, or make a batch of green buttercream frosting (recipe can be found on page 13).

Using a piping bag or a frosting tool of your choice, place a green border around the entire cake pan. We like to use the frosting tip that has all the little holes in it so it looks like grass.

Tear open a sheet full of marshmallow Peeps® and add a thick line of frosting to the back. Place them in your desired position (the frosting back will keep them from falling off) then use candy chocolate eggs or jelly beans to decorate.

Peeps® Pizza

The Little Princess Punch

Now I'll bet most of you don't know who the heck Shirley Temple is, but if you're in the mood for some nostalgic classic film viewage, you should really check out The Little Princess. Believe me, kids, it was a classic back when I was a classic... you know, back when TVs had tubes in them, and there was only one per household! Can you imagine? This recipe is a twist on the classic Shirley Temple drink that only your mom will remember, but it doesn't mean you can't enjoy it, too!

WHAT YOU WILL NEED:

½ **CUP** Pineapple juice
1 BOTTLE Sprite, 7-up, or lemon-lime flavored soda
1 JAR Maraschino cherries (you'll need the juice)
1 QUART Raspberry sorbet

THE STEP BY STEP:

In a large pitcher, stir together the ½ cup pineapple juice, Sprite, and ¼ cup juice from maraschino cherries.

Pour into champagne glasses until they're about three-fourths full, then add 1 scoop raspberry sherbet and top with a cherry. This is the prettiest and most dramatic way to serve it, as it will foam beautifully once you add the sherbet, but beware: its Instagram-worthiness overflows into messiness quick!

For less mess, add sherbet to the pitcher and let melt before serving.

Dirt Worm Pudding Pie

We used to go digging for worms in the garden every Saturday morning in the summer so Dad would have bait to go cat-fishing on the Mississippi. My little sister and I would scream (in both joy and terror) as we sang "Nobody loves me, everybody hates me, I eat worms all day! First I bite the heads off, then I spit the guts out, then I throw the skins away!"

During those long, hot Iowa summers, we would invite the neighborhood kids over, dye our spaghetti lunches red and blue, and try heartily convince everyone in the neighborhood that we truly ate worms!

However, there is absolutely no need to be grossed out or throw any of this magical concoction away. Because Dirt Worm Pie is simply the most amazing way to eat worms today. This delicious treat will have kids both squirming and begging for more! So pull up a spoon (or a shovel) and dig in!

EASY BAKE OPTION:

Tell your dad you're sick and the only cure is dirt worms. Then simply sit back and enjoy.

Dirt Worm Pudding

WHAT YOU WILL NEED:

¼ **CUP** Butter, softened

1 BLOCK 8 oz. cream cheese, softened

1 CUP Powdered sugar

3 ½ CUPS Milk

2 PACKAGES 3.5 oz Instant vanilla pudding

1 TUB 12 oz Cool Whip®, thawed

20 COOKIES Oreo® cookies work best, crushed finely

20 PIECES Gummy worms

THE STEP BY STEP:

STEP 1　Mix ¼ cup butter, 1 block of softened cream cheese, and 1 cup powdered sugar in a large bowl till it becomes a beautiful creamy mixture.

STEP 2　In a second large bowl, mix 3 ½ cups milk and 2 packages vanilla pudding together till it starts to feel slightly firm, like pudding. Then stir in the entire tub of Cool Whip®.

STEP 3　Combine the two bowls, and stir until completely mixed.

STEP 4　Layer mixture into a bucket or clear bowl and top with crushed Oreos and gummy worms.

DECORATING TIPS:

We like to serve Dirt Worm Pudding in a large sand buckets with shovels. For a party, we like to lay out a large plastic tablecloth with napkins and dump the bucket right in the middle, then decorate with Oreo® cookies and worms all around.

For individual servings, use clear plastic cups and sandwich the worms between layers of crushed cookies and pudding.

If the vanilla flavor is too boring for you, substitute it with 2 packages of instant chocolate pudding instead!

Dirt Worm Pudding

Circus Monkey Munchies

The circus hardly ever came to our town, but when it did my parents would always try to get seats in the bandstand. The Barnum and Bailey Circus was a treat. For many of us, it was the first time we had ever seen exotic animals like elephants, monkeys, and tigers. The whole town would show up, stuffing their faces with pink cotton candy, popcorn, and tangerine circus peanuts.

Walking into the big top tent was a show all unto itself! The clowns, the flamethrowers, and the monkeys tumbled into my little sister's and my dreams for the entire summer... so, needless to say, we two monkeys also worked that deep magic into our kitchen in the form of this powdered sugar treat!

EASY BAKE OPTION:

Go to the local store and pretend you're a monkey till your neighbors fill up your basket up with treats. LOL.

Circus Monkey Munchies

WHAT YOU WILL NEED:

9 CUPS Rice Chex™ Cereal

1 CUP White chocolate chips

½ CUP Peanut butter

¼ CUP Butter

1 TEASPOON Vanilla extract

1 BOTTLE Small, round rainbow sprinkles

1 ½ CUPS Powdered sugar

THE STEP BY STEP:

STEP 1   Put 9 cups of Rice Chex™ in a large bowl and set aside.

STEP 2   In large microwaveable bowl, microwave 1 cup white chocolate chips, ½ cup peanut butter, and ¼ cup butter for 1 minute; stir. Then microwave for another 30 seconds or till the mix is able to be stirred smooth. Add vanilla extract and pour the entire mixture over Rice Chex™. Add small, round rainbow sprinkles and pour into a large plastic bag.

STEP 3   Add 1 ½ cups powdered sugar to the large bag and shake until well coated. Add more sprinkles and lay on waxed paper.

STEP 4   Let cool, and serve.

DECORATING TIPS:

Want to make your Circus Monkey Munchies extra special?

For a neat fall or Halloween treat, use semisweet chocolate chips (instead of white chocolate chips) and add Reese's Pieces®, peanut butter cups, and pretzels. Your guests will go berserk for the amazing concoction of peanut butter flavors.

You can also make it a rainbow treat by adding M&M's® and pretzels for extra color. We like to serve this confection on rainbow napkins, but you could also serve it in a large white bowl.

Circus Monkey Munchies

Peanut Butter Egg Baskets

Obviously holidays that revolved around candy were a big hit in my house. So as soon as Easter rolled around, the kids were twitterpated by my mom's favorite springtime peanut butter cup classic. This treat is supereasy to make and perfect for all your colorful egg-hunting egg-stravaganzas.

WHAT YOU WILL NEED:

1 CUP Light corn syrup

1 CUP Sugar

1 CUP Peanut butter

6 CUPS Rice Krispies® cereal

1 CUP Semi-sweet chocolate chips

THE STEP BY STEP:

Combine 1 cup corn syrup and 1 cup sugar in large pot or saucepan. Place the pot over medium heat, stirring frequently, until sugar dissolves and begins to boil. Remove from heat and stir in 1 cup peanut butter.

Add 6 cups Rice Krispies® cereal and stir until everything is covered. Spray cooking spray over a cupcake pan and begin to scoop the mix into the cups.

Melt 1 cup chocolate chips in pot over low heat, stirring constantly, then spoon over the cups of cereal. Let cool and decorate with buttercream and Reese's® Peanut Butter Eggs.

Poo Party Cupcakes

Yup, this one is B-A-N-A-N-A-S! And we love it. Just as the poo emoji has captured the hearts of mainstream culture, it has also captured the hearts of our kitchen. Emojis are the 21st-century hieroglyphs of our generation. I hope hundreds of years from now, when aliens or future civilizations dig up the remains of pop culture, they are truly perplexed and in awe of how we communicated our deepest feelings of excitement and joy with poo!

Poo Party Cupcakes are our new favorite way to celebrate! They're an instant party starter, adorable, and extremely delicious. To make them, we turned to my grandmothers time-honored recipe for Midnight Cake, and whipped it into a 21st century emoji masterpiece! Our grandmothers would probably be shocked and appalled, but our hats are off to them for inspiring our creative hearts and cultivating our love for baking, no matter what shape it ends up taking!

EASY BAKE OPTION:

Recipe can be substituted with a box of Devil's Food or basic chocolate cake mix. Then decorate with canned chocolate frosting from the store!

Midnight Cake
with Poo Party Chocolate Frosting

WHAT YOU WILL NEED:

2 CUPS Sugar

2 LARGE Eggs

1 TEASPOON Vanilla extract

1 ¾ CUPS Self-rising flour

¾ CUP Cocoa powder

1 ½ TEASPOONS Baking powder

1 ½ TEASPOONS Baking soda

1 TEASPOON Salt

½ CUP Canola Oil (or vegetable oil)

1 CUP Milk

1 CUP Hot water (boiling)

THE STEP BY STEP:

STEP 1   Preheat the oven to 350°F; meanwhile in a large mixing bowl, cream together 2 cups sugar, 2 eggs, and 1 teaspoon vanilla extract and beat with a hand mixer for 2 minutes.

STEP 2   Gradually fold into the wet mixture 1 ¾ cup flour, ¾ cup cocoa, 1 ½ teaspoons baking powder, 1 ½ teaspoon baking soda, and 1 teaspoon salt.

STEP 3   Add ½ cup oil, and 1 cup milk, stir, and mix in 1 cup hot water. You can place the water in the microwave for 2 minutes, or until it boils. Don't worry, the batter will be thin. It's fine.

STEP 4   Prepare cupcake tins with liners, then pour batter into cupcake form, filling a little over halfway and bake for 20 minutes, (If making a cake, grease, flour, and fill two 9-inch cake pans or bake for 30 minutes.) Make sure that cupcakes cool completely before frosting.

POO PARTY CHOCOLATE FROSTING:

⅔ CUP Cocoa powder

3 CUPS Powdered sugar

½ CUP Softened butter (or Crisco)

1 TEASPOON Vanilla extract

5 TABLESPOONS Milk

Put ⅔ cups cocoa and 3 cups powdered sugar in a large mixing bowl. Then add ½ cup softened butter (or Crisco) to the bowl, followed by 1 teaspoon vanilla extract and run on low till they start to mix.

Keep mixer running and add 5 tablespoons milk slowly, until frosting is thick. If your frosting becomes too stiff, add more milk.

Add frosting to a piping bag (or frosting tool of your choice) and use a large tipped circle to apply the frosting in a slow rolled swirl forming a cone shape on top of the cupcake.

DECORATING TIP:

Use Wilton® mini candy eyeballs or pre-made fondant icing to create the emoji character eyes and mouth.

Jurassic Sugar Cookies

My grandmother's classic sugar cookies are the one recipe for which she will be most remembered. I can recall spending countless days in her kitchen rolling out dough as thin as we could make it, cutting the most perfect shapes into its soft surface, and gently transferring them to baking sheets. Even after all this time that she has been gone, my sister, my mom, and I still have Grandma's cookie cutters in our kitchens.

I am sure Grandma would have loved my favorite new dinosaur cookie cutters that I will no doubt pass down to future generations of our family... because surely nothing could make Grandma's already-epic cookies more so than going Jurassic. Finding the remnants of a Tyrannosaurus Rex (even in cookie form) is a serious delight to many budding archaeologists; perhaps it might even inspire the dreams of the next Jurassic DNA-splitting entrepreneurs!

EASY BAKE OPTION:

Recipe can be substituted with Pillsbury® roll-out sugar cookies. Be sure to chill dough for 1 hour prior to rolling out. For the best results, roll dough out thin.

Jurassic Sugar Cookies

WHAT YOU WILL NEED:

1 ½ CUPS Sugar

½ CUP Butter (or margarine)

½ CUP Crisco

3 LARGE Eggs

1 TEASPOON Vanilla extract

3 ½ CUPS All-purpose flour

2 TEASPOONS Baking powder

1 TEASPOON Salt

1 TEASPOON Nutmeg (or cardamom, optional)

THE STEP BY STEP:

STEP 1   Preheat oven to 350°F. Then in a large mixing bowl, combine 1 ½ cups sugar, ½ cup butter, ½ cup Crisco, 3 eggs, and 1 teaspoon vanilla extract. With a hand mixer, beat until creamy.

STEP 2   Using a large wooden spatula, add in 3 ½ cups flour, 2 teaspoons baking powder, and 1 teaspoon each of salt and nutmeg. Stir until dough forms a firm ball.

STEP 3   Place the dough ball in a large bowl, cover in plastic wrap, and place in the freezer for 2 hours or overnight.

STEP 4   Take out the chilled dough and break in half, place between 2 pieces of parchment paper, and using a rolling pin roll thin.

STEP 5   Loosen the parchment paper by pulling it away from the dough, place gently back on dough, then flip and repeat.

STEP 6   Cut into shapes and bake for 10 minutes, or until golden.

ROYAL ICING:

3 LARGE Egg whites
4 CUPS Powdered sugar
1 TABLESPOON Water (as needed)
1 BOTTLE Food coloring

In large bowl, combine the egg whites and beat until frothy. Add powdered sugar slowly and mix with a hand mixer on high, beating until mixture forms stiff, glossy peaks. This can take up to 5–7 minutes. Add water and food coloring as needed.

DECORATING TIPS:

Scoop icing into bag or small bottle with a fine tip. Then trace the entire edge of your cookie first and fill in the middle. The outline edge should harden and allow the inside to flood.

Add sprinkles as desired.

Jurassic Sugar Cookies

North Pole Sundae

This hometown treat is from my favorite pizza parlor and ice cream shop, "Happy Joe's"—or, as we liked to call it in high school, "Gay José's!" We would wait all year for the December ice cream special, which was always the North Pole Sundae! And from December to January we would eat more ice cream than we did all summer!

WHAT YOU WILL NEED:

Peppermint or Vanilla Ice Cream
Marshmallow Topping
Hot Fudge
Whipped Cream
Peanuts
Candy Canes, crushed
Maraschino Cherries

THE STEP BY STEP:

Fill a large white cup (or sundae glass) about halfway full with peppermint ice cream. Top with a layer of marshmallow creme and hot fudge.

Continue to fill the cup to the top, adding another layer of both marshmallow creme and hot fudge before topping the glass with whipped cream, peanuts (if desired), and crushed candy canes.

Don't forget to add a cherry on top, and a candy cane stick (or two) for some winter flair!

Frosty's Chocolate Fever

Let me tell you, Frosty and I have one thing in common, a bad case of Bieber Fever! But I am fairly certain that I have seen our boy in concert more times than my melted friend here... he just can't ever seem to make it to the arena in one piece. But for those snowy winter days when we can't spend each moment with Justin, me and Frosty sure do know how to reminisce over an amazing cup of dark chocolate cocoa with a very Biebs holiday album.

WHAT YOU WILL NEED:

3 ½ CUPS Sugar
2 ¼ CUPS Cocoa powder
1 TABLESPOON Salt
1 CUP Whole milk for serving

THE STEP BY STEP:

In a large mixing bowl, combine 3½ cups sugar, 2 ¼ cocoa powder, and 1 tablespoon salt, and whisk to combine well. Store in a plastic container or jar until ready to use.

In a ceramic mug, add 1 cup of whole milk and microwave on high for 1 minute or until hot. Add 2 tablespoons of cocoa mix, and stir to dissolve.

FROSTY MARSHMALLOWS:

Grab a bag of large marshmallows, cut in half, and lightly coat the back with powered sugar so they don't stick. Then decorate with Royal Icing (recipe on page 55) in black and orange, or store-bought gel frosting will work just as well.

Hypercolor Chex Mix

You won't remember 1989 like Taylor Swift and I remember 1989, but trust us the t-shirts were cool and we were stylin'. Hypercolor tees would change color when they came in contact with heat, so needless to say my little sister and I had more than a few fights with the hairdryer that year. That memory still brings a smile to my face and inspired this melted multicolor Chex mix!

WHAT YOU WILL NEED:

1 BOX Chex™ Mix or plain Chex™ cereal (10.5 oz.)
1 BAG Butter-flavored waffle pretzels (9 oz.)
½ CUP Each candy melts - pink, yellow, green, blue & purple
1 BAG Rainbow M&M's®
1 BOTTLE Rainbow sprinkles (optional)

THE STEP BY STEP:

Spread Chex™ Mix and pretzels on a baking sheet lined with parchment.

Arrange candy melts in rainbow order on a 9-inch microwave-safe baking dish. Microwave on high in 30-second spurts until candy becomes soft and melted.

With a spoon, gently stir each color to soften, then drizzle over a small portion of the pretzel mixture. Sprinkle with candies and sprinkles before drizzling the next layer of color. Then once the candy melts have set, gently break up the mixture into bite-sized chunks. Serve and enjoy!

Coffee Shop Doughnuts

Sundays were hectic in Iowa, as we all rushed around the house slipping on our best church clothes and trying to scoot out the door before Dad was hollering at us to get a move on.

Secretly it wasn't that hard for us to get our butts in gear because we knew if we moved fast and stayed well-behaved during the Sunday mass, we would be rewarded. On the corner across from my church, there was a Doughnut Hut, and if my little sister and I could keep it together while the priest droned through the homily, we knew Dad would pick up a dozen frosted and glazed doughnuts for the ride home.

Needless to say, Jesus may have been in our hearts on Sundays, but doughnuts were on our mind.

EASY BAKE OPTION:

You can substitute this recipe with a box of pancake mix. Make as directed on the box, just add 2 tablespoons canola oil and 2 tablespoons sugar. Bake 10 minutes and pick up at the decorating tips on the next page.

Coffee Shop Doughnuts

WHAT YOU WILL NEED:

2 LARGE Eggs

¼ CUP Softened butter (or Crisco)

½ CUP White sugar

⅓ CUP Brown sugar

1 TEASPOON Vanilla extract

1 ½ TEASPOONS Baking powder

¼ TEASPOON Baking soda

1 TEASPOON Ground nutmeg, to taste

¾ TEASPOON Salt

2 ⅔ CUPS Self-rising flour

¼ CUP Canola oil

1 CUP Milk

THE STEP BY STEP:

STEP 1   Preheat the oven to 425°F. Lightly grease two standard doughnut pans.

STEP 2   In a medium-sized mixing bowl, beat together the 2 eggs, ¼ cup butter (or Crisco), ½ cup white sugar, ⅓ cup brown sugar, and 1 teaspoon vanilla extract until smooth.

STEP 3   Stir in 1 ½ teaspoons baking powder, ¼ teaspoon baking soda, 1 teaspoon nutmeg, ¾ teaspoon salt, and 2 ⅔ cups flour.

STEP 4   Then add ¼ cup canola oil and 1 cup milk into the butter mixture and beat with hand mixer until everything is combined.

STEP 5   Spoon the batter into the lightly greased doughnut pans, filling the wells to about ¼" shy of the rim.

STEP 6   Bake the doughnuts for 10 minutes. Remove them from the oven, and wait 5 to 7 minutes before turning them out of the pans onto a rack.

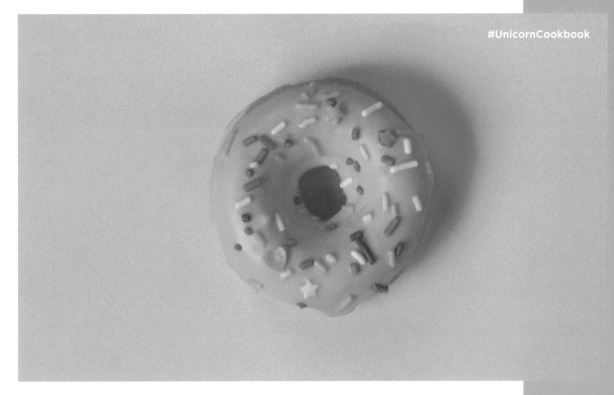

DECORATING TIPS:

We decorated these delicious doughnuts by dipping the tops in pink Royal Icing (recipe on page 55) and covering in a melange of rainbow sprinkles, stars, and hearts.

Simply take the doughnut by hand and dip the top into your bowl of Royal Icing. Turn the doughnut clockwise until the top is completely covered. Set aside on a cooling rack and apply sprinkles generously.

For chocolate chip doughnuts, stir in ¾ cup chocolate chips into the batter before following the rest of the instructions and decorating accordingly.

Coffee Shop Doughnuts

Unicorn Hot Cocoa

When I was a kid, nothing was cooler than arriving at school decked out with a Lisa Frank Trapper Keeper®! (Look it up, kids.) And so it's no wonder that on early fall nights after countless hours spent collecting technicolor leopards and unicorns stickers, we'd sit down to make a cup of hot chocolate inspired by Lisa's legendary influence.

WHAT YOU WILL NEED:

4 CUPS Milk
1 CUP White chocolate chips
1 TEASPOON Vanilla extract
1 TEASPOON Salt
1 BOTTLE Americolor fuschia food coloring

THE STEP BY STEP:

In a large saucepan, combine 4 cups milk, 1 cup white chocolate chips, 1 teaspoon vanilla extract, and 1 teaspoon salt. Then, over medium to low heat, stir continuously until the white chocolate has melted and the mix is smooth; don't boil. Add 1 or 2 drops of fushcia food coloring and stir.

Top with whipped cream, colored marshmallows, and sprinkles!

EASY BAKE OPTION:

Recipe can be substituted with Land O' Lakes Classic Arctic White Hot Cocoa Mix. Then add a drop or two of fuschia food coloring to each cup and decorate.

Starlite Cake Pops

Saturday mornings were for watching the adventures of Red Butler and Shy Violet unfold as they danced around with their friends Starlite and Rainbow Brite.

While Rainbow's best friend Twink was mining Star Sprinkles in the caves of Rainbow Land, my sister and I were creating colorful confections to match in the kitchen.

WHAT YOU WILL NEED:

4-5 CUPS White cake (we save and use our leftover cake tops)
3 TABLESPOONS Buttercream frosting (see page 13 for recipe)
10 STICKS Lollipop sticks
5 BAGS Candy melts, all colors

THE STEP BY STEP:

In a large bowl, mix leftover cake tops with a 3 large tablespoons of buttercream frosting. With your hands, clump and roll the mixture into balls and freeze for one hour.

In a microwave-safe bowl, melt colored candy melts in the microwave, stirring every 30 seconds. Then dip your lollipop stick into the melted chocolate up to one inch. Then shove the chocolate covered stick into the frozen cake ball and dip into the melted chocolate, spooning chocolate over the entire ball and gently tapping off the excess back into the bowl.

Immediately top with sprinkles and spin cake pop in your hand for 30–60 seconds while blowing, allowing the chocolate to harden.

Rainbow Cake Nirvana

True enlightenment may be hard to come by, but this seven-layer piece of heaven will help at least your tastebuds get there. The first time I ever made a rainbow cake was with my mother for my 37th birthday. It was a behemoth, and it toppled over when we cut into it. Devouring the beautiful mess was the best way to celebrate the end of such an elegant creation.

Often in baking—as in life, actually—we find that the point is not so much the end product as it is the journey you took to get there. My journey through the years in my mother's kitchen with my brothers and sisters has been a loving endeavor I will carry with me forever, toppled cakes and all.

Sometimes done is better than perfect, and sometimes perfect is a matter of how you look at it. From my kitchen to yours, may all your rainbow-colored kitchen adventures be an absolute smash!

EASY BAKE OPTION:

You can substitute for the following recipe 2 white cake box mixes instead. For the best colors, follow the box directions but substitute whole eggs for egg whites, adding 1 extra egg white per mix.

Rainbow Cake Nirvana

WHAT YOU WILL NEED:

4 LARGE Egg whites

2 CUPS White sugar

2 TEASPOONS Vanilla extract

2 CUPS Self-rising flour

4 TEASPOONS Baking powder

1 TEASPOON Salt

½ CUP Vegetable or canola oil

1 CUP Milk

1 CUP Hot water (boiling)

7 BOTTLES Americolor food dye 7 rainbow colors

THE STEP BY STEP:

STEP 1 Preheat the oven to 350°F; meanwhile in a large mixing bowl, beat 4 egg whites with a hand mixer. Then slowly add 2 cups sugar, and 2 teaspoons vanilla extract and continue to beat for at least 3 minutes.

STEP 2 Gradually fold into the wet mixture 2 cups flour, 4 teaspoons baking powder, and 1 teaspoon salt.

STEP 3 Add ½ cup oil, and 1 cup milk, stir, and mix in 1 cup hot water. You can place the water in the microwave for 2 minutes, or until it boils. The batter will be thin, this is ok.

STEP 4 Split the batter evenly into four bowls and add a different color dye to each bowl. You will need to make this recipe twice to get all 7 layers, so you will end up with extra batter.

STEP 5 Grease four 6-inch cake pans and bake for 30 minutes or until the tops become golden brown.

DECORATING TIPS:

Freeze cakes for at least 1 hour. Then take the chilled cakes from the freezer and begin to level your cake. You can use a long, serrated knife to carefully cut the tops off your cake. (Save the cake tops for our cake pop recipe on page 67).

Using a traditional buttercream (recipe on page 13), stack each layer of your cake and apply piped frosting in between each layer. Flatten with an offset spatula, making sure to add more frosting than you think you need. It's much easier to remove icing at a later point than it is to add it. It's okay if the frosting overflows; you can use it to coat the outside of the cake.

Start adding icing to the sides of the cake, and use your free hand to turn the cake to apply the frosting evenly. When you are done with frosting the cake on all sides, go back a second time and make sure the top and sides are smooth.

Place the cake in the freezer and allow to harden (overnight or at very least for 1 hour). Then decorate the smooth cake with colored frosting and candy. I like to pipe pink florets all over the top for added fun!

Rainbow Cake Nirvana

Candy Heart Cheesecakes

He loves me, he loves me not. He loves me, he loves me not. Actually, who cares?! We love you!

Forget boys on Valentine's Day and spend it with your best bunch of gal-pals. My partner, the Fairy Boss Mother, loves to call Valentine's Day "Galentine's Day" because it's one of the best holidays to celebrate your truest and deepest friendships.

Love is all around you on all days; why only celebrate the ones that we play kissy-face with? These mini-cheesecakes are the perfect things to bake up for your next Galentine's Day party, so invite your squad over and celebrate in style!

EASY BAKE OPTION:

Conversation Hearts are the best way to express your truest feelings. So text your closest gal pal to come over and help you cook, because this recipe is a little harder and takes some extra work—just like relationships.

Candy Heart Cheesecakes

WHAT YOU WILL NEED:

1 CUP Graham cracker crumbs (15 squares)

1 TEASPOON Sugar with a pinch of cinnamon

¼ CUP butter, melted

2 BLOCKS Cream cheese, softened (16 ounces)

1 CUP Sugar

1 PINT Sour cream (16 ounces)

1 TEASPOON Vanilla extract

3 LARGE Eggs

FOOD COLORING Pink, purple, blue, green, yellow, and red

THE STEP BY STEP:

STEP 1 Fill a roasting pan with enough water to come halfway up the sides of silicone heart molds. Set pan in oven and heat oven to 325°F.

STEP 2 In a medium bowl, mix together 1 cup graham cracker crumbs, 1 teaspoon sugar/cinnamon mixture, and ¼ cup melted butter. Then divide the graham cracker crumbs among the 12 heart-shaped molds.

STEP 3 Press the crumbs into an even layer and refrigerate.

STEP 4 Beat 2 blocks of softened cream cheese until smooth.

STEP 5 Add 1 cup sugar to the cream cheese and beat until combined.

STEP 6 Mix in 1 pint sour cream, 1 teaspoon vanilla, and 3 eggs, then beat until creamy. Divide the mixture into bowls and add color.

STEP BY STEP CONTINUED:

STEP 7   Take your heart molds from the freezer and evenly add the colored filling to each container.

STEP 8   Place the cheesecake molds in a water bath and bake for 18-24 minutes. If the center is wet when you do a toothpick test, continue to bake for 3–5 more minutes.

STEP 9   After you've removed the cheesecakes from the oven, lift them from the water and cool at room temperature for an hour and a half.

STEP 10   Freeze for at least two hours, placing a paper towel on top to collect moisture, then remove from molds.

STEP 11   Add red food coloring to our Royal Icing (see recipe on page 55), then frost conversation-heart phrases onto the tops of the cheesecakes.

Candy Heart Cheesecakes

Grandma's Grasshoppers

My grandmother lived 15 miles outside of our town on a small country road in a tiny town of just 20 houses and a single church— Rickardsville, Iowa. Summers were full of sleepovers, card games, and swinging on the big porch swing under the giant weeping willow in her yard. Grasshoppers would fly through the tall grass and fields, and my grandma would always joke that she caught them and served them up to us in milkshakes.

This glass of Crème de Menthe-flavored ice cream swiftly takes me back to her house on warm summer days with my cousins all screaming for grasshoppers!

WHAT YOU WILL NEED:

1 QUART Vanilla ice cream
1 CUP Milk
1 BOTTLE Crème de Menthe flavored syrup
1 BOX Chocolate cream cookies / Oreos®
1 BOTTLE Chocolate syrup

THE STEP BY STEP:

Combine into a blender 1 quart of ice cream, 1 cup of milk, and two tablespoons of Crème de Menthe flavoring. Add 5 Oreo® cookies and blend on high for 3 minutes. Add more milk if mixture is too thick.

Coat the inside of a tall glass with chocolate syrup and pour green ice cream mix inside. Top with whipped cream, cookie crumbs, and sprinkles, of course!

Cupcake Ice Cream Cones

As luck would have it, I was a summer baby, and my birthday party was always also an end-of-the-school-year celebration. Some of my favorite memories include all the kids from my class coming over and playing Red Rover while we fished for treats with poles out the kitchen window. Best of all, I'll never forget my favorite neighbor lady, Mrs. O'Brien, always made her amazing Cupcake Ice Cream Cones for the celebration each summer.

WHAT YOU WILL NEED:

1 BOX Ice cream cones, wafer style
1 BOX White cake mix
1 BATCH Buttercream frosting

THE STEP BY STEP:

Preheat the oven to 350°F. Then get started on your cake batter: you can use the recipe on page 16 or instead purchase any box cake mix from the store and follow the instructions on the back of the box. Next place 12 ice cream cones standing tall on a baking tray, and fill each cone about ¾ th of the way up with cake batter.

Place in the oven for 18-20 minutes or until the tops are golden brown. Decorate with buttercream frosting (recipe on page 13), piling it high up in a cone shape, and generously apply sprinkles .

Glass Slipper Mirror Glaze

One of my favorite memories as a kid was when we would run through the house, parading after our mom with a basket full of laundry, pretending to be little mice singing the work song from Cinderella. "Cinderelly, Cinderelly, night and day it's Cinderelly! Make the fire, fix the breakfast, wash the dishes, do the mopping! We can do it, we can do it, we can help our Cinderelly." And although we were never very good at getting our chores done on time, we did learn a lot about how to help mom make some excellent Cinderella magic in the kitchen.

So when leaving a ball and cascading down the front steps, be sure to leave the prince an excellent cake topper, and grab a slice of this royal dessert for the carriage ride home. Believe me, my family's Midnight Cake (see recipe on page 50) with Glass Slipper Mirror Glaze is the stuff of fairytale dreams.

Growing up in Iowa was the start of my Cinderella story. The magic created there inspired me to start Cinderly, my grown-up company, so I could keep making magic everyday!

EASY BAKE OPTION:

Sorry, guys, this is pretty much the hardest one in the book! But at this point you've earned your seasoned fairy godmother wings, so give it a whirl!

Glass Slipper Mirror Glaze

8 TEASPOONS Unflavored powdered gelatin (¾ ounce)

1 ¼ CUP Water (divided use)

1 ¾ CUPS Sugar

½ CUP Sweetened condensed milk

1 TEASPOON Vanilla extract

¼ TEASPOON Salt

2 1/2 CUPS White chocolate chips

3 BOTTLES Food coloring, white, dark blue, and sky blue

THE STEP BY STEP:

STEP 1   Stir gelatin and ½ cup warm water in a bowl and let sit 5 minutes.

STEP 2   In a large sauce pan gather 1 ¾ cups sugar, ½ cup sweetened condensed milk, 1 teaspoon vanilla extract, ¼ teaspoon salt, and ¾ cup water over medium heat, stirring occasionally until mixture begins to bubble, about 4 minutes. Add gelatin mixture, and stir until dissolved.

STEP 3   Remove from heat and add chocolate chips, stirring constantly, until melted. Strain through a fine-mesh sieve into a large bowl, then divide glaze among 3 bowls. Color each with food coloring as desired. We dyed ours dark blue and sky blue, then left one white.

STEP 4   Let cool, stirring occasionally to stop skins from forming, until glazes are cool enough to touch (90°F), about 10–12 minutes.

STEP 5   Pour half of first glaze into a large bowl, then pour half of second glaze into the center, followed by half of third glaze. Repeat to form circles of different colors in bowl.

STEP BY STEP CONTINUED:

STEP 6   Place your chilled, crumb-coated cake on a cake pan or an overturned bowl set inside a rimmed baking sheet or large tray to catch drips. Pour colored glaze over the cake, sweeping back and forth across cake to form a marbled pattern.

STEP 7   Resist the temptation to touch the glaze once it's poured; it will start to set as soon as it hits the cold cake. Let glaze drip about 10 minutes, then clean up edges with a small offset spatula or butter knife.

STEP 8   Transfer cake to a serving platter and chill for at least 30 minutes.

Glass Slipper Mirror Glaze

KICKSTARTED BY THESE AMAZING PEOPLE:

Alex Tabino, Frannie Strober Cassano, Stacie Laufenburger, Dina & Lea Mara, The Creative Fund, Stacy Balk, Rachel Stein, Kimberly Hale, Laura Kawano, Eve Himmelheber, Nicolaj Jensen, Lisa Catto, Connie Koorevaar, Andrew Jeffries, Michael Binegar, Bart Decrem, Sarah Little, Lesley Maio, Paul Nixon, Nik Estes, Hilary N. McNeill, Eliana Louise Marcellene Rodgers & Lindsey Rodgers, Audrey & Andrew Briggs, Lily Nyman, Emilee Janikowski, David Ameer Tavakoli, Beth Nizack, Geoffrey Potgieter, Kelly Goeke, Penelope Haymore, Jens Kaiser, Sandra Pride, Nansi Schneider, Fran Monopoli, Jessica Lyons, The Braskat-Arellanes Family - Caradwen, Cruz III, & Cruz IV, Lisa Tegels, Daniel Beaver-Seitz, Erin Clark, Sarah Fuentez, Traci Eichhorst Holloway, Calliope Carroll, Laney Russell, Katelyn, Pat Eichhorst, Digitalis Collective, Cindy I., Krissy Potter, Cara Kovalovich, c4studio, Mary Margaret Crocker, Bailey Ader, Suzzette, Michael John & Adeline McDonough, Bridgette Magee, Derek Boudreaux, Amanda Meyer, Hector, Lauren Webber, Winter Jackson King, Carrie Pozdol, Kate Nintzel, Tommy Kleckner, Elaine R. Latta, Shane Tilston, Jill Connors, Laurie Eustis, Angela Lyon Briggs, Kristin Carlson, Adam Lance Garcia, Erica Rotstein, Drew J Simpson, Laura von Holt, Bluesette Copeland, Isabel Seymour, Michayla Daleydolloff, Julia Arazi, Eve & Will Wolff, Nicole Eichhorst Swanson, Stephanie Mustain Gulizia, Anne Bown-Crawford, The Knight of Void, Judy Acosta, Philip Hale, Nicholas Bown-Crawford, Patricia Ray, Kaylen Hann, Allison Martin, Vas Fury, Melanie Houselog, Arianna & Laurence Shapiro, Layla Fingleton, John Moody, Jennifer Hill, littleladyvader, Kenneth Watson, Julie Undem, Patricia Jenatsch, Eve Underwood, Deanna Shoup, Sarah Easter, Tyler Duncan, Margo Weaver, DiveDog, Paula Stewart, Anne Z, Michael Kivetz, Luke Galambos, John Cryderman, Kaylah Valaquez, Amanda Jaskiewicz, Charis, Ken Shannon, Lisa Sustaita, The Lawrance Gals, Reina M Knight, Shannon Broderick, Icis Machine, Mirabelle Johanna Peng, Ronald Olufunwa, Christiana Phinney, Erika Johnson, Alvin, Andrea Merritt, Madelynn J. Kendrick, Stacey Voyles, Rayanna, Lily & Ivey Perry, Daniel Latarski, Mayumi Shimose Poe, Lostmartyr, Jon Clark, Kammie Fenwick, Sarah Ashley, Danielle Martel, Rebecca Walter, Vreni Meier, Reggie Raupe, Bex, Jen M, Ekster Family, Peyton Zusmer, Darra Zankman, Acholi Southerland, Evelyn Moss, Tanya Miller, Thomas Kuil, Erin McIntyre, Sir Knight Meow, Gracelyn Stevenson, Steven Carrillo, Jalin Wilcox, Emily Shurtliff, Blue Rose Jewels, Elizabeth Shurtliff, Sam and Al Walkowiak, Joulelee, Keira Long, Ashley Wright, Hannah Lennerz, Liz Hopkins, Steven Barrie, Margaret M. St. John, Samantha, Robert Vreeland,

Benjamin Ortiz Jr, Annabat, Richard & Amy Martin, Celeste Maisel, Kellan Peterson, Lacey Jade Fogliaro, Malena Farrell, Paul Abbott, Olivia and Jannah, Phrixus, Patricia Copeland, Emily Purvis, Carolee Flatley-Scott, The Brush Family, Dale, Heather Moraw, David Ballard, John McGrath, Will Donovan, Steve Hoeker, Jessica Ayers, Pancakes and Toast Guhlers, Amy White, Lara Frick, Tess McElreavy, Orri Leví Úlfarsson, Joseph Thibault, Mickey McKimm, Brooke Knipper, Kbuendicho, Tiffany Cross, Jessica Ayers, Marylou Lacuesta Holly, John Le Drew, Emily Mulcahy, Silke Rau, Katie Shuter Rompala, Kristina Hoge, Josh Porter, Eric Harlacher, stephfh, Ole Sandbæk Jørgensen, Jenn and Eleanor, Vickie Stoffel, Khaliah Williams, Elizabeth Taylor, Stella Whitenack, Torbjørn Moe Johansen, Namtran Nguyen, Jeremy Cabana, Isis Valk, Barbara Alcorn, Daniel O'Connell, Ali Kartiganer, Anonymous, Earl Scott Mouton, Daniel C, Michael H. Gossage, BOUTIN Maxime, Liza Vercruyssen, Adam F. Goldberg, Charlene Cuaresma, Zaza D, Victoria, Trevor A. Ramirez, Heather Moody, Devi Cassandra Monjot, Kay Clopton, Brendan, tematim, Jaclyn Ciamillo, Nathan Homb, Kari Wilbanks, Leisha Montrosse, Mary Galeti, Dennis Aras, Helen Febrie, Elizabeth Bastyr, Christa, LenNoG, Vaibhav Puranik, Alex Wiesen, Angela Pastrana, Bob Covey, Danni, Lisa Manna, Daniel Dhearnmedhakul, Jessica Mae Leuenberger, Adam Parker, Marc Schaerer, Dante Cammarata, Jesse Kimmel-Freeman, David Ruskin, Tim & Jessica Wheaton, Shea Russell, Vinnie Harned, Ember Zimmerman, Aidan Tardif, Layla & Daisy Basso, Tabby Queenie-Ann, Gwyn Risley, Jon Klein, Aurora Wallis, Joyce Stoffel, Cristina, The Lopez Family, Corrina Reimert, Alice Healy, Caroline Duvier, Cathy Mullican, Ross Williams, Nicole Ross, Jessie Wray Caknipe, Marlee and Weezie Brand, Toby Steevenson, Zac Holden, Christina Spoljaric, Ken McGuire, Regina Head, Tierra Smith, Jason Smith, Bala Ramanujam, Sergey Anikushin, Mary Wolf, Lynne Clark, Sarah Hoff, Miranda Smith, Sraddha Patel, Jay Parsell, Julia Winter, Michael Gale, Brad Roberts, Antony Wright, Kerilyn Micale, Michelle Grondine, Katie Stotler, Brooke Griffin, Stephanie Magin & Prosecco Giro de Ombre.

For a list of our kitchen accessories visit:
www.unicorncookbook.com

THE END

cinderly

www.unicorncookbook.com